"MAKING IT IN SPITE OF..."

THE JOB
THE SYSTEM
THE ECONOMY
THE CUSTOMER
THE BOSS...!

and

THE SELF

"MAKING IT IN SPITE OF..."

THE JOB
THE SYSTEM
THE ECONOMY
THE CUSTOMER
THE BOSS*...!*

and

THE SELF

BY

J. THOMAS MILLER, III

ISBN: 1-58820-070-1

1st Books Rev. 9/28/00

FORWARD

In twenty seven years as a business consultant and management development specialist, I have arrived at this conclusion: ***individual failure is due more to negative attitudes and misperceptions than all other causes combined.***

THUS:

This book will help the reader correct both attitudes and perceptions regarding:

THE JOB
THE SYSTEM
THE ECONOMY
THE CUSTOMER
THE BOSS...

AND THE *"SELF"* AS WELL

The purpose of this book is to assist every reader...whether employee, supervisor, or chief executive... to become aware of one great fact; ***being employed is both the greatest gift and the greatest responsibility a person can enjoy.*** A further goal is to make every reader a winner...***ONE WHO MAKES IT IN SPITE OF...!***

NOTE

If you plan to read only one book this year to help yourself, this is the book to read!

WHY YOU SHOULD READ THIS BOOK!!! BENEFITS TO THE READER

** The book will **replace negative and defeating attitudes** with positive and winning attitudes.
** The book will give the reader a greater appreciation for **their role** in their success through **emphasizing the importance and dignity of work.**
** The book will **correct the notion** that work is **only** a means to an end.
** The book will **enforce the truth** that work is honorable, meaningful, and **is one of our most important stages** for self development and self expression.
** The book **will provide** the reader with a greater feeling of being an ***important*** part of their organizational team.
** The book will **instill** in the reader the fact that the one who ***makes it in spite of...***is that person who has a ***commitment...***not just a job.
** The book will **induce** the reader to understand a set of attitude options that, when acted upon, will give the ultimate in ***job security...being more needed by the organization than they need the organization...!***

*"MANY RECEIVE
ADVICE,
ONLY THE WISE PROFIT FROM IT."*

Syrus

DEDICATION

TO CARMEN FOR HER
WISE COUNSEL

TO MY CHILDREN
MIKE, JEFF, STEVE & LISA
WHOSE BELIEF IN ME
HAS MORE THAN ONCE KEPT ME ON TRACK

MY GRANDCHILDREN
JUSTIN & CASSIDY & ALEX
FOR WHOSE FUTURE WE WORK TO MAKE BETTER
THAN OUR PAST

*TO THOSE COUNTLESS MILLIONS WHO DAY BY DAY
PERFORM THE TASKS DUTIES AND
RESPONSIBILITIES THAT MAKE LIFE RICHER FOR US
ALL...*

INTRODUCTION

Each day countless millions journey forth to the **world of work**. For some it is an easy walk to the barn, for others it is a brisk jaunt from the apartment to the office, for still others it is a grueling two hour commute on a crowded freeway. Regardless of how they travel, they **will** arrive at their place of EMPLOYMENT for the performance of their daily tasks duties and responsibilities.

For eight or more hours they will interact with ,THE BOSS, THE SYSTEM, THE ECONOMY, FELLOW WORKERS, THE CUSTOMER, THE JOB AND WITH THEMSELVES. In short, they will have much about which to form attitudes . And the attitudes they form will make them or break them...the attitudes they form will allow them to ***make it in spite of...***or be defeated at every turn of the road.

Attitude is defined as: *"A state of mind or feeling with regard to some matter."*

From this definition it is clear that our attitude determines our outlook and our outlook determines the nature of our actions and activities toward anything in life: Family, friends, self, religion, and most especially work. The list is endless. The conclusion is fact...A POSITIVE ATTITUDE YIELDS POSITIVE ACTION AND POSITIVE RESULTS...A NEGATIVE ATTITUDE YIELDS NEGATIVE ACTION AND NEGATIVE RESULTS.

*SIMPLY STATED...**THE ATTITUDES WE HOLD MAKE US OR BREAK US!!***

In order to be among those who **make it in spite of...** it is vitally necessary to mold and hold attitudes that allow the **best of you** to be in every phase of life. Seek to be a winner and avoid at all cost being a loser...**the attitude you hold is the key to the difference, as illustrated by the following:**

WINNER VS. LOSER

The Winner ---is always part of the answer;
The Loser ---is always part of the problem;
The Winner---always has a program;
The Loser ---always has an excuse;
The Winner---says "let me do it for you;"
The Loser---says "That's not my job;"
The Winner---sees an answer for every problem;
The Loser---sees a problem for every answer;
The Winner ---sees a green near every sand trap;
The Loser---sees two or three sand traps near every green;
The Winner---says, "It may be difficult but it's possible;"
The Loser---says, "It may be possible but it is too difficult."

BE A WINNER...!

AUTHOR UNKNOWN

This writer certainly realized the potential of a positive attitude. This author knew the value of seeing the problems but not dwelling on them. The message is clear, problems exist but for every problem there is also an opportunity. The difference of whether or not the problem overwhelms the opportunity is in the ATTITUDE of the observer.

The single most distinguishing factor in those who ***MAKE IT IN SPITE OF*** *is their ability to* ***turn every problem into an opportunity through an attitude adjustment from negative to positive. <u>This book will point out the needed adjustments and how to make them!!!</u>***

THE EVIDENCE

The quest for ***winners*** is universal. American business and industry spend **mega money** annually in their desire to establish a winning spirit in their organizations. In this never ending search for **quality, excellence, and an increase in individual productivity** there has emerged program after program: (TQM-Total Quality Management) ... (JIT - Just In Time) ... (SPC-Statistical Process Control) ... Team Building ... Employee Empowerment ... Total Employee Involvement ... Participative Management ... Quality Circles ... DDI ... The Ropes Course Training ... Desert Kings ... and a whole host of others as beneficial as these ...!

HOWEVER

THERE ARE STILL TOO MANY INDIVIDUALS WITH NEGATIVE ATTITUDE PROBLEMS!

It is the sincere hope of the author that many of these negative attitudes will be addressed and suggestions made to give the holder of the attitude, an alternative way to think in a more positive and productive manner...!

J. THOMAS (TOM) MILLER, III
LEADERSHIP SEMINAR ASSOCIATES
610 Elberta Lane
Ft. Mill, S.C. 29715
TELEPHONE (803) 396-8275

MAKING
IT
IN SPITE OF....

THE JOB
THE BOSS
THE SYSTEM
THE ECONOMY
THE CUSTOMER
AND
THE SELF !!!

SECRET--!
ENJOY WORK
FOR THE WHOLE OF HUMAN HISTORY
AND PROGRESS
IS WRITTEN IN OUR ABILITY
TO PERFORM MEANINGFUL WORK---!

TABLE OF CONTENTS
DEFEATING ATTITUDES & ADJUSTMENTS

TABLE OF CONTENTS
DEFEATING ATTITUDES & ADJUSTMENTS

ATTITUDE PROBLEM

"IT'S JUST A JOB"

It was early winter. The builder had finally completed his first housing development. We stood on a hill overlooking the fifty or so new houses his company had constructed. The air was cold and crisp and still. The smoke from open fireplaces was rising from chimneys into the clear early evening air.

As I reflected on the scene I remarked, "Just think of the contribution you have made. You have provided homes where the warmth and love of families will be nurtured. Thanksgiving will be celebrated. Christmas will be observed and children will grow to adulthood and life will be enjoyed. You should be very proud of this accomplishment."

He looked at me and said, "Are you crazy? This damn thing nearly killed me."

His focus, was on the problems, not the beneficial end. The result: ***"it's just a job syndrome."*** It is a shame. He made money, but he missed out on the larger reward...the feeling of having made life better for others.

SUGGESTED ATTITUDE ADJUSTMENT

LOOK FOR THE GREATER GOOD

There is no such thing as "just a job." All jobs have in the performance of their function something that makes life better for someone, somewhere.

The essence of work satisfaction is a feeling of personal contribution. *In order to truly appreciate the work we do and its value, we must develop THE ATTITUDE that our work does something to make life better for others.* The person who *makes it in spite of... never focuses on the problems. Rather, they focus on the contribution they are making for the benefit of others.*

The person who is really ***"MAKING IT IN SPITE OF"*** has a commitment...not, "just a job."

Illustration: Jane cleans offices at night. Her major motivation is the extra money she earns in order to send her son to college. Being a night maid for an office may be, to some, demeaning work. However, not only does Jane earn for her son's education, she also provides a service that enhances office morale through cleanliness and order. When made aware of the deeper meaning of her job...she now leaves fresh flowers!

ATTITUDE PROBLEM

"IT'S NOT MY JOB"

"That's not my job"...is a story about four people named Everybody, Somebody, Anybody and Nobody. There was an important job to be done and Everybody was sure that Somebody would do it. Anybody could have done it, but Nobody did it. Somebody got angry about that, because it was Everybody's job. Everybody thought Anybody could do it, but Nobody realized that Everybody wouldn't do it. It ended up that Everybody blamed Somebody when Nobody did what Anybody could have.

TRUTH: If you never do more than you get paid to do...you will never be paid for more than you do.

SUGGESTED ATTITUDE ADJUSTMENT

ABOVE THE CALL OF DUTY

RESPONSIBILITY

Where your job or organization has a problem or a need and you have the talent to improve it or to make it better, that is where you are called to act whether it is part of your job description or not.

Those who are "**Making it in spite of**"...live by the definition of responsibility written above. They make things better for all. Instead of avoiding responsibility and the tasks and accountability that go with it, they **seek out** opportunities to make a real contribution and to increase their own productivity for the good of the total work place.

ATTITUDE PROBLEM

"JUST GETTING THROUGH THE DAY"

Many times we have heard someone say, "If I can just get through the day."

This is the attitude of the bored. They have the tendency to waste the time of the really busy people. Their whole demeanor is one of boredom. The woeful fact is that they are missing out on all the opportunities afforded them by being on the job. They want only to "serve their time" and go home.

SUGGESTED ATTITUDE ADJUSTMENT

GET INVOLVED

The Person who suffers from the "just get through the day" attitude because they are bored with their job needs to understand that, for most, the only excitement in almost any job is the excitement the person performing that job brings to it.

The truth is that not many people have jobs which are inherently exciting. Few have the work adventure of an "Indiana Jones." or a James Bond 007. However, all of those who enjoy employment do have a stage upon which to become excited. The employee who is "**Making it in spite of" understands the truth of the fact that sometimes the greatest adventure in work is in a simple, job well done!**

Illustration: John was a summer employee. He was working the summer between graduation from high school and entering college in the fall. He worked in the tool room for the construction company that had hired him. In the morning he issued the crews their tools for the day. In the afternoon he checked the tools back in. The afternoon check in sometimes took an hour or more. John took it upon himself to devise a system that cut the check in time to minutes. This reduced the waiting time for everybody. John was never formally recognized for his contribution...but he knew he had made a positive difference and for him, that was enough. He got involved. He created his own job excitement.

ATTITUDE PROBLEM

"I JUST WORK HERE"

This phrase when used to a customer, or a fellow employee, is a dead give-away that the person who said it feels they are not a member of the team. Rather, they perceive themselves as being just a cog in the wheel and not an individual contributor to the organization's on-going success.

This statement is also a certain indication to anyone that the "I just work here," employee is not going to assume the responsibility to aid the customer or a fellow coworker or the organization solve any problem. However, the "I just work here" attitude shows conclusively that such individuals are perfectly willing to pass the responsibility for all helpful actions along to someone else.

SUGGESTED ATTITUDE ADJUSTMENT

BECOME AN INTEGRAL PART

In order to be one of those rare individuals who are "**making it in spite of**", you must understand your vital part as a member of the team and act on this understanding.

A troubled customer, fellow employee or organization is looking for help, guidance, direction, or anything to address and / or solve their problem.

Solving the problem may not be immediately possible but the person with the "**making it in spite of** " attitude will listen attentively, and take the responsibility to offer constructive suggestions, point out new directions, show an attitude of interest, and think through the situation so they might give valuable and valid comments to address the concerns faced by those in need of assistance.

ATTITUDE PROBLEM

"SOMEONE ELSE WILL TAKE CARE OF IT"

Persons who suffer from this attitude problem do not know the meaning of the word initiative.

These persons leave everything to somebody else.

They miss out on the joy of ever being the first with the most.

Unfortunately this attitude problem allows it's victim to watch while others do. They sit on the side line while everybody else is in the game.

IF IT NEEDS DOING-DO IT

Outstanding performance is recognized when one actively seeks ways to extend one's self.

An oil slick on the shop room floor may be the janitors job to clean up but it is surely impressive to management and to fellow employees when there is that person who extends themselves to clear the hazard to help the whole group...whether it is their job or not.

Someone else will always take care of most things that need attention. However, those who are "**making it in spite of**", are the ones who look for ways to help the group...they know the truth of the statement, "**Everything is possible if you don't care who gets the credit.**"

This doesn't mean volunteering. Volunteers are those who are asked. Here I am speaking about the individual who does something extra just because it needs doing.

ATTITUDE PROBLEM

"THE BOSS IS AN IDIOT"

Sometimes...but few and far between...unfortunately this is true. A case in point was the new maintenance supervisor who was meeting for the first time with his crew to have a personal get acquainted interview. One member of his crew was an individual whose name was Jose' Stein. Jose' was of both Mexican and Jewish heritage. In the interview the first thing the supervisor said to Jose' was, "Jose' do you know who are the two most dangerous people in the world?" Jose', trying to be cooperative replied, "No, who?"

The supervisor then said to Jose', "A hungry Jew and a Spic with a spray can."

This was an idiotic, insensitive thing to say and a certain way to create an unbridgeable gap between himself and Jose'. To say the least, that supervisor did not last long in the organization.

Without doubt such incidents do happen between supervisor and employee, but they are **the exception ...not the rule.**

SUGGESTED ATTITUDE ADJUSTMENT

REMEMBER THAT "NOBODY'S PERFECT!!!"

The vast majority of bosses are sensitive, caring, and interested in their employee's welfare. They want to help the members of their team to succeed.

The attitude of the employee should be not only to be managed by the boss but to manage the boss as well. The rule of thumb for the employee to manage the boss is three fold:

1. Make your boss look good!
2. Keep your boss informed of both the good and the bad...in reality, all crap should not flow only down hill!
3. Maintain the integrity of your duties and responsibilities!

Realize: If you will make your boss a king or a queen ... your boss will keep you a prince or a princess ... and for most of us that is enough.

ATTITUDE PROBLEM

"THE SYSTEM IS STUPID"

A system is a combination of rules, regulations and procedures that give order to the process of running a business. Systems give an order to the day to day operation of the enterprise.

The person with the attitude of the system is stupid looks for ways to beat it, ways to subdue it and ways to keep from conforming to it. Theirs is a constant battle of wits to win by subduing the established procedures and programs.

They dissipate their strength, concentrate on the wrong results and **become rebels without a real cause.** They seek personal aggrandizement and wind up being considered as those who can't be trusted and always seek the short cuts. Ultimately they fail both themselves and their organization.

DETERMINE TO MAKE THE SYSTEM BETTER

That person who is "**making it in spite of...**" is the person who is determined to make the system better for everybody. It is true that they can see the flaws in the procedures that are hampering the progress of the organization...but they don't fight them. Rather, what they do is to initiate changes that will make the system better. They seek to initiate a system that will streamline, modernize, simplify, and increase efficiency for the whole.

Dissatisfaction with the system should breed change...not complaints...creativity, not negativism.

The person who is "**Making it in spite of**" understands that systems should serve people not people serving the system.

ATTITUDE PROBLEM

"BUILDING MY KINGDOM IN MY LIFETIME"

The person with this attitude breeds self-centeredness and the using of others for personal gain. They also live by a spirit of manipulation not motivation.

To the individual with this attitude their most important focus is how they will benefit from the efforts of others. Regardless of what others do to enhance the life of the organization these persons will find a way to steal the credit for themselves.

Their downfall will be in the fact that others will begin to "see" through them and to isolate them.

The person with this attitude will ultimately fail because they will not be able to succeed alone and on their own.

SUGGESTED ATTITUDE ADJUSTMENT

GIVE CREDIT WHERE CREDIT IS DUE!!!

The talent to inspire others, spur them to greater achievement, accomplish goals and overcome obstacles is the true mark of leadership. The person who can do this is that individual who puts goal attainment first, appreciation of others efforts second, and self last.

These are the people who "**make it in spite of...**" because they have an attitude of goals first, self second. They believe in the old adage "give the credit where the credit is due."

Theirs becomes the exalted position of being the person with a power others freely give them, and they are the, or one of the most powerful persons in the organization. Why? Because they have given credit where credit was due. They seek success for themselves...but they also actively seek to make others successful.

ATTITUDE PROBLEM

RESENTMENT

Resentment is defined as, "Anger or indignation over something held to be wrong or unfair."

Resentment unchecked will create chaos in the life of the person doing the resenting and in the organization of which that person is a part. Resentment quickly destroys a relationship and causes an undercurrent of ill will. Persons who allow resentment to rule in their life soon find more and more situations to resent because resentment poisons the spirit.

Maintaining an attitude of resentment takes energy. In order to be the best we can be at all times so we can **make it in spite of**, we need all the positive energy we can muster. Because resentment breeds bitterness, resentment has no place in the experience of the person who is really seeking to be all they can be.

Most negative of all, the person eaten alive with the attitude of resentment will be sapped of their enthusiasm, making the words of ***H.W. Arnold most appropriate says Arnold:***

"The worst bankrupt in
the world is the person who
has lost his enthusiasm."

SUGGESTED ATTITUDE ADJUSTMENT

RESENTMENT RESOLUTION TAKES GUTS

To reduce resentment it is often necessary to confront the situation and / or the behavior that is the cause for the resentment in the first place. Most situations and / or behaviors that create resentment do so because they produce a feeling of powerlessness. The holder of the resentment does so because they feel they are being treated wrongly or unfairly or they feel they are being victimized by a situation over which they feel they have no control or influence...in short they feel they are being DONE TO...!, thus they resent their plight.

The only answer here is confrontation...the airing of the truth as they see it. Confrontation to discuss situations or behaviors that cause resentment are rarely pleasant, but, unlike resentment they are usually temporary and result in constructive change.

Illustration: In a small office with a staff of five, one of the staff consistently takes advantage of the relatively low structured office environment. In the view of the others they take every opportunity to take time off, come in late, leave early, and leave their duties to be covered by someone else. However, in filling out their time sheet they claim a full forty hour duty week whether or not this was indeed the case. The office manager seems unwilling to control the situation. In the meantime resentment and its negative effect grows in the rest of the staff. Unfortunately this will be the case until someone forces the issue to resolution. **After all, resentments can't be bygones until the cause for the resentments is a bygone.**

ATTITUDE PROBLEM

SEEKING REVENGE

The seeking revenge attitude is akin to, but far exceeds, the "getting even" syndrome.

The desire for revenge when strong enough becomes the main motivation for all of a persons activities and energies. Their major thrust is to seek to hurt, to damage, to wreck, to impede, to harm and to maim the object of their revenge. The creative juices that should be focused and flowing to further their career, make contributions to their organizations and **make it in spite of**, are, instead, diluted to the negative tunnel vision of making someone suffer.

To live for revenge is one of the greatest tragedies in life.

SUGGESTED ATTITUDE ADJUSTMENT

"FORGIVE AND FORGET"

Revenge!!!. It is doubtful that any living human being above the age of consent has not felt the desire for revenge. However, thank God, more revenge impulse goes controlled than uncontrolled. The attitude of "forgive and forget" is the attitude of a much bigger person than those seekers of revenge.

Courage is always greatest when blended with meekness; intellectual ability is most admired when it sparkles in the setting of a modest self distrust; never does a human soul appear so strong as when it forgoes revenge and dares to forgive any injury.

Thomas Fuller wrote, ***"Doing an injury puts you below your enemy; revenging one, makes you even with him; forgiving it sets you above him because the noblest revenge is to forgive."***

As has been indicated earlier in the book, the person who is **making it in spite of...**is set apart and functions with a positive not negative attitude. Rene' Descartes was such a person and his attitude toward revenge is reflected in his statement, "When anyone has offended me, I try to raise my soul so high that the offense cannot reach it."

ATTITUDE PROBLEM

HOSTILITY

If you are the holder of this attitude, please know that all those around you would rather be somewhere else. Why? I'll tell you why. They are suffering from "egg shell shock."

What do I mean? Simply this, they feel they must walk as if on egg shells to keep your mouth from attacking them. The person who suffers from the ***hostility attitude*** makes all around them feel they must be very careful in what they do and say else they will cause you to unleash your caustic comments in their direction.

At best the chronic **hostile attitude** will be met with ,"just consider the source" tolerance.

At second best the chronic hostile attitude will be confronted with the same hostility they display. At the very worst the chronic hostile attitude person will be treated with indifference...i.e. they will become non persons to those around them. Their only social contact will be the result of necessity, never choice.

In isolation none of us does very well. The very best way to insure our isolation is to hold and to display an attitude of hostility.

COOPERATION WORKS BUT HOSTILITY ISOLATES...

The person with a hostile attitude treats others as if they were enemies. The person, however, who is **making it in spite of** understands that they are dependent on others for success. Working with others means that we can accomplish far more than we can in isolation, imposed by hostility. Therefore, to gain cooperation, cooperate!

John F. Wharton put it this way, "If one man is an expert fisherman, and another an expert at handling a boat, the two working together will catch twice as many fish as either working alone. This principle of specializing is important for anyone to understand when he seeks to earn a living."

"How extraordinary is the situation of us mortals. Each of us is here for a brief sojourn; for what purpose he knows not, though he sometimes thinks he senses it. But without going deeper than our daily life, it is plain that we exist for our fellow men, in the first place for those upon whose smiles and welfare our happiness depends, and next for all those unknown to us personally but to whose destinies we are bound by the tie of sympathy. A hundred times every day I remind myself that my inner and outer life depend on the labors of other men, living and dead, and that I must exert myself in order to give in the measure as I have received and am still receiving." Albert Einstein

ATTITUDE PROBLEM

AGGRESSIVENESS

The person who is suffering from the attitude problem of **aggressiveness** is best described as a "bull in a china shop."

In their eyes their only place is the center of attention. Theirs' is the only right way and they are chronic fault finders.

The aggressive person sees their behavior as a show of confidence, however, others see them as obnoxious, pushy and demanding, with razor sharp ***TONGUES***.

Waiters and waitresses, bell hops and hotel desk clerks dread to see them coming. Family members and coworkers have as little to do with them as is possible.

Their aggressiveness leads to boistriousness...and they often wonder why "everyone is so stupid." The end result is, they spend a lot of time alone. The pity is, they do not realize why!

SUGGESTED ATTITUDE ADJUSTMENT

"BLESSED ARE THE MEEK"

To be meek is not to be bland or weak. To have the attitude of meekness is to be sure of one's self and to show the strength of true confidence. The meek know who they are, and they know their own worth and value so, they don't have the need to aggressively, constantly remind others of their self importance.

Contrary to what we might think, this person is rarely taken advantage of because they exude a quiet confidence that shouts to all who come into contact with them, "I am somebody!"

These people will **make it in spite of** because they treat everybody as if they are somebody as well!

ATTITUDE PROBLEM

NEGATIVISM...!

These are the people that you know God created to make your life miserable upon this earth!! These are the people whose attitude is to point out what they deem is wrong with everything and they waste no time in telling you. However, they can't tell you how to "fix" anything. They try your patience, raise your blood pressure and seek to throw a wet blanket on everything you suggest.

They never see "half full", but they always see "half empty." These are the people whose lives are dominated by "should's and ought's." They try as best they can to impose their should's and ought's on everybody.

Those who hold this attitude never see the possibilities but they always see the problems.

They retard creativity, frustrate progress and miss out on the new, the different and the exciting. Theirs is never **making it in spite of, rather theirs is, "I didn't make it because of...!"**

SUGGESTED ATTITUDE ADJUSTMENT

LOOK FOR THE POSSIBILITIES

For the person who is **making it in spite of**...anything is possible. What can be is limited only by the imagination of the thinker. They believe anything is possible. They know there is a way over, under, around, or through any obstacle.

They do not fear confrontation or negativism. In every situation they look for the new, the different, the possible. They understand that what was truth yesterday is a lie today and what is truth today will be a lie tomorrow.

For the person who looks for the possibilities the horizon is endless...and they will **make it in spite of** because they are not limited to the past...theirs is the ability and the commitment the make the future today!

Join the ranks of those with vision and make it happen!!! This is the attitude that wins, this is the attitude of those who will **make it in spite of...!!!**

GOSSIP

For some reason we like nothing better than to talk about each other. In every organization rumors abound. We want to know who has "pull" with whom, who is dating whom, who is "sleeping" with whom. Unlike communication which is "the passing of information and understanding", gossip is the passing of hearsay, innuendo, and false information. The more sensational the gossip, the more "juicy" it is to the recipient, and the more likely they are to pass it on.

Those who freely engage in gossip seldom think of the fact that they often pass "stories" that will do irreversible damage to the reputation and the character of those who are the subjects of their tales, true or not.

Sooner or later the gossip bearer will be isolated, cut off, and deprived of information. They will be seen as the one not to be trusted.

Worse than this, the chronic gossip is often used as a vehicle to feed the grapevine what others want known but do not desire to be identified as the one's passing the "stories."

SUGGESTED ATTITUDE ADJUSTMENT

"TURN A DEAF EAR"

When confronted with the open gossip of the woman caught in adultery, Jesus said it best, "Let you who is without sin caste the first stone." If you remember the story in the Gospel of John, no stone was thrown. With this simple but profound statement He turned a deaf ear to the accusations and put everything into true perspective.

Who among us could withstand a microscopic investigation of our behavior. We are all candidates for stories in the "National Inquirer."

We are people first and behaviors second. Those who will **make it in spite of** are those who focus on person first...behavior second. They believe about others only what they experience. ***They turn a deaf ear to gossip and give everyone the benefit of the doubt.***

The person who **will make it in spite of** remembers the old Indian saying, "Do not judge your brother until you have walked two miles in his moccasins."

"We cannot control the evil TONGUES of others ; but a good life enables us to disregard them.." Cato

ATTITUDE PROBLEM

CHRONIC ANGER

There are those persons who display chronic anger...they are abrupt, they are rude, and they display little, if any, feeling for others. Theirs is the "get even for what the world has done to me attitude." Their whole goal in most problematic situations is to **place blame**. Blame for their failures. Blame for their mistakes. Only secondarily do they focus on solving the problem. These persons react with ***too frequent irritation***. In fact, it seems as if everything in some way irritates them and ***nothing pleases*** them. After a while, they get what pleases them, ***nothing!***

Chronic anger will "eat you alive." Anger negatively effects judgement and makes for tension, leads to over reaction and when acted upon impulsively, will often create ***undue stress and/or IRREVERSIBLE*** heartbreaking situations both in business and personal life.

When I was in military school I was a Cadet Major. One day I observed a Platoon leader really dressing down one of his squad leaders. When he was finished I took him aside and asked, "What happened?" The Lt. replied, "He screwed up on purpose Major, I just had to give him a piece of my mind." Then I remembered what the wise M/Sgt. R.O.T.C. instructor had said to me when he had observed me doing the exact same thing. "Miller", he had said, "Don't give away so many pieces of your mind that you don't have enough left for yourself." Then he walked away. I've never forgotten it. I passed it on to the Lt. and, like the Sgt., walked away.

Note to the manager and supervisor...when an employee reduces you to the DISPLAY of inappropriate anger...<u>you lose!</u>

SUGGESTED ATTITUDE ADJUSTMENT

"COOL IT OR CHILL OUT"

There are some situations and conditions for which anger is truly an appropriate response.

World hunger is an anger evoking situation, man's inhumanity to man should surely bring forth anger. Cruelty, abuse, manipulation, the using of people instead of utilizing them are all reasons for anger. Anger is a very human emotion. Jesus became angry with the Money Changers in the Temple and He acted on it. His anger ***was appropriate to the situation. One of the best revelations of true character is what you allow to make you angry.***

When a person stops and thinks about it...***there are only a few things in everyday life*** worth really making you angry. The rule of thumb is this:

(1)--If it doesn't effect your marriage...
(2)--If it doesn't effect your family...
(3)--If it doesn't effect your money...
(4)--If it doesn't effect your job...
(5)--If it doesn't effect your mail...

WHY GET ANGRY?
Just "Chill Out !!!"

After fifty years of a near perfect marriage which had pretty much been void of argument or anger the husband was asked what had made their great success. Thinking for a moment he answered thoughtfully, "I believe it was our agreement on decision making. I made all the decisions on big things, world peace, government policies, national budget space program. She made the decisions on everything else, you know, the little things."

ATTITUDE PROBLEM

"BACK BITING"

The "back biter" is loathed. Theirs is the habit of making others look bad so they can look good.

Only "little" people are back biters.

Back biters are those who do what they do to spite others...they will never make it **in spite of...**!

Back biters soon discover, often too late, ***those bitten, bite back, but not in the back.***

SUGGESTED ATTITUDE ADJUSTMENT

RESOLVE

Resolve

to be "bigger" than

back biting

then

you will **make it in spite of...**

EVEN YOURSELF!

Make it in spite of by being ***honest, truthful, forthright and open*** in your relationship with yourself and with others. Those who do this often find they don't have to worry about their back...somebody is covering it.

ATTITUDE PROBLEM

INATTENTION TO DETAIL

This person's motto is, "let it slide." To the person with this attitude someone else is responsible to see to it that "there is a place for everything and that everything is in it's place."

Since accuracy is the last thing they think of or are interested in, everything they do must be checked for conformance to standards. They are often the cause of costly mistakes.

Illustration: The customer service rep took the call. The established customer ordered 4,000 boxes. The customer service rep wrote one zero too many. This changed the order to 40,000 boxes. No attention to detail by anyone in the production chain cost the manufacturer 36,000 boxes. A costly mistake.

Unfortunately such situations happen all to often.

SUGGESTED ATTITUDE ADJUSTMENT

ATTENTION TO DETAIL REVEALS CHARACTER

Mistakes may be a part of life and living but for the person who **makes it in spite of** those mistakes will be far and few between. They live by what Martin Luther King, Jr. expressed so well:

"If a man is called to be a
street sweeper, he should sweep streets
even as Michelangelo painted,
or Beethoven composed music,
or Shakespeare wrote poetry.
He should sweep streets so well
that all the hosts of heaven and earth
will pause to say, 'here lived a great
street sweeper who did his job well'."

THOUGHT: One of the best ways to **make it in spite of** is to **cover the honest mistakes of others...especially if it is a mistake that the boss has made.**

ATTITUDE PROBLEM

"QUALITY IS SOMEONE ELSE'S JOB"

Very simply put...quality is...doing the job right the first time. That person who holds the attitude of quality is the job of "quality control" or "engineering" or anyone but themselves is a person who is not living in the reality of today, the reality of today is that quality is the most important aspect of life be it in work or in personal relationships.

They have the attitude of "**close is good enough.**"

Their work is sloppy, their car is a mess, their yard always needs attention. They have never even entertained the notion that "little things mean a lot."

These are never the one's who **make it in spite of** because they only do that which is acceptable to "get by."

For whatever unfortunate reason, **they lack pride in themselves and in a "job well done."**

SUGGESTED ATTITUDE ADJUSTMENT

"QUALITY IS EVERYONE'S JOB"

In spite of standards, in spite if inspection, in spite of statistical process control, in spite of total employee involvement, in spite of quality circles...**real quality happens only when the individual doing the work has a pride in themselves...**and perceives the correctness of their labor as an extension of their own worth and value.

The person who produces quality efforts does not do it for the company, or the customer, rather, they do it for themselves!

Will A. Foster is correct in saying:

> "*Quality is never an accident;*
> *it is always the result of high*
> *intention, sincere effort, intelligent*
> *direction and skillful execution;*
> *it represents the wise choice of*
> *many alternatives.*"

QUALITY PRODUCTS, GOODS AND SERVICES RESULT FROM THE EFFORTS OF QUALITY PEOPLE!!!

ATTITUDE PROBLEM

"ANYTHING TO GET OUTTA'HERE"

Not long ago I was searching for a gift for my wife for her birthday. I was in one of the shops in the mall. As I browsed, one of the sales persons offered to help. She appeared bored. Her assistance seemed forced and instead of making suggestions about the available choices she only responded to my questions. She was dutifully polite, responsive and helpful...you know, **kind of robotic.**

My selection being made, I gave her the credit card for payment. As I reached for the card my airline ticket fell from the inside coat pocket. She asked if I was about to take a trip. I told her "yes, to Los Angeles." Then she remarked, "I wish I had a job that required travel...**anything to get outta' here.**"

It was a revealing statement. It gave me the probable cause of her **robotic attitude.** She just didn't like her job and it showed.

I wondered what their repeat customer rate was. I knew I wouldn't be back.

SUGGESTED ATTITUDE ADJUSTMENT

LOVE WHAT YOU DO

People who love what they do are spontaneous, enthusiastic, outgoing and helpful. These are the people who make suggestions, reflect an interest in both their jobs and others.

Katherine Graham put
it
this way:

"To love what you do and
feel that it matters---
how could anything be
more fun?"

Try to develop the attitude of, "I can't wait to get in to work," and let the "I'd give anything to get outa here," attitude go. You will like it better and so will everyone else. If you find that this positive attitude is impossible to develop in your present job, then do yourself and your company a favor, do anything necessary to get outta' there and find another job.

ATTITUDE PROBLEM

"I'M POWERLESS"

"I'm powerless", is the attitude of the person who, when faced with a challenge or a crisis or a tough decision, will do nothing because they feel there is nothing they can do. They are unwilling to take risk. They do not realize that you can't steal second with your foot on first. The idea of initiative is alien to them and they **are powerless, but only because they perceive themselves as being without power.**

This often leads to their being taken advantage of by others. They recognize the injustice but do nothing about it, again, because they feel there is nothing they can do.

The following saying is appropriate to the person who feels powerless:

***"The man who believes
he can do something
is probably right, and
so is the man who believes
he can't."***

The person whose attitude is that they have no power mistakenly feels power comes only to those in positions of power.

SUGGESTED ATTITUDE ADJUSTMENT

ESTABLISH A PERSONAL PURPOSE

The whole of human history makes valid the fact that personal power is in direct proportion to personal purpose. As Victor Hugo put it:

***"There is one thing
stronger than all the
armies in the world,
and that is an idea
whose time has come."***

The feeling of the lack of power in one's life is usually associated with the belief that 'things' in one's life are insurmountable because there is no evident way of how to overcome them.

But history proves that if there is a firm 'what' in mind, the difficulty in the 'how' will be overcome. Or one will endure almost any 'how' for the realization of a chosen referent goal enactment.

Remember, power does not come only by position or intellect or even money. Power comes from our capacity, and while we may not have equal position or equal intellect or equal money ... we all have capacity. Your power will come in realizing yours to its fullest.

ATTITUDE PROBLEM

"IT'S SOMEONE ELSE'S FAULT"

Persons with this attitude are an enigma. They do not fail to take risks, initiate, or act, but when something goes wrong, and it usually does, it is always someone else's fault.

Since these people will never admit they are wrong or that they made a mistake, they never accept the 'blame'. They seem unable to tolerate even the mildest forms of criticism, and when confronted with the possibility that they have made an error, there is usually an unreasonable display of temper and outrage and indignation. These persons are chronic seekers of ways to make others their scapegoat.

They give the outward appearance of helpfulness, however, their real goal is to control. To the work force of which they are a part, they are disruptive, rude, disrespectful, and caustic...especially when they are disagreed with.

Since there is no admission of wrong doing, or fault...there is no correction of their behavior.

They are difficult to live with, work with, and relate to, because when others are trying to resolve problems with them...the second it appears they are to be 'blamed', their favorite saying is, "the conversation is over because it's not my fault anyway." Who do they think they are fooling?!

SUGGESTED ATTITUDE ADJUSTMENT

MISTAKES ARE OPPORTUNITIES FOR GROWTH!!!

One of the major marks of true maturity is the ability to accept the fact that, as page 12 indicates, "Nobody's Perfect.", not even ourselves.

The person who is "**making it in spite of**" understands that it takes a much bigger person to admit an error than to doggedly deny the possibility that they could have made one. It is a fatal mistake in any relationship, be it personal or business, never to admit, "I'm wrong."

"**Making it in spite of**", means earning the respect and trust of others through the free admission and acknowledgment of errors. Those who hold this attitude understand , "To err is human, to forgive is divine." They also know it is essential to look at ourselves in this light.

All errors when recognized, realized and acknowledged, are learning experiences. You see, negative learning can and does create personal growth when the attitude allows it.

Observed mistakes of self and others are learning experiences...***i.e. what not to do.***

WORKING FOR MONEY ONLY

Most people have experienced the anxiety of personal financial flux, that ebb and flow of money. Most would certainly agree that having money is more desirable than not having it. However, when the acquisition of money is the central focus of life there is a loss of involvement in all the rest.

Relationships suffer, marriages fail, and children become strangers. Values become distorted and perspectives are limited to the narrow margin of "progress resides only in profit." These persons are prone to compromise not only their own ethics and integrity but that of their company, organization or enterprise as well. Therefore, people with whom they do business, both coworker and customer, soon begin to mistrust their word and the money they seek with such passion evades them and the vicious cycle starts over again. The "working only for money " individual will gain the reputation of the person who will "do anything for money."

Unfortunately, the working only for money also gives a false sense of success they think they have made a success of life, when all they have made is just a lot of money. Somewhere along the way they overlooked the fact that money lost can be replaced, but time lost is gone forever!

SUGGESTED ATTITUDE ADJUSTMENT

KEEP MONEY IN PERSPECTIVE

It is true that the vast majority of those of us who work for a living do just that, work for a living. In return for the tasks, duties, and responsibilities we perform and we earn a designated amount of money. In our culture money is the medium of exchange we use to acquire those things necessary to make, maintain and increase a standard of living.

For those who **make it in spite of** money is just that , a medium of exchange...***money is the means not the master***. Money is important but not to the exclusion of all things else.

Those who **make it in spite of** realize the only real security a person can have in this world are the resources of knowledge, experience and ability judicially utilized with ethics and integrity to make this world a better place for all. ***To such people money comes!***

To those who **make it in spite of** money is a good provider when its acquisition is only a part of life and living and they exert every reasonable and honest effort to earn it. They will not, however, "sell their souls" to have it.

The best perception of money is; money is a tool, it should never be an obsession!

ATTITUDE PROBLEM

WORKING FROM FEAR OF LOSS MORE THAN HOPE OF GAIN

Each day millions of workers walk through the doors of their work place with a subliminal fear gnawing at their guts ... "If I mess up today I might be fired." These are those millions of persons who dislike their jobs and know a better way to perform them but they are afraid to voice their opinions because they fear they might be fired.

These persons are working more from the fear of loss than the hope of gain. As a result they are controlled by fear and inhibited in their ability to initiate constructive suggestions for changes that would make the whole operation better. What they would lose if their suggestion offended someone and their job taken away is a sure thing. What they may gain should their suggestion be accepted is only a hope.

Thus, theirs is the plight of all too many who, because of necessity, must work to provide but do not enjoy what they do because what they do is less than their potential. This condition creates an attitude of futility, frustration, desperation and despair. This situation also creates an army of employees who work more because they are afraid not to than because they are highly motivated each day to perform their daily routines. Instead of **making it in spite of** they will be defeated because of...!

Their job is important to them, but they don't feel important to their job.

SUGGESTED ATTITUDE ADJUSTMENT

GO FOR IT...!

Adopt the attitude of "go for it"...remember you were looking for a job when you found the one you have now. Life is too short to spend one third or more of it feeling as if you were a "thing", an "it" or a "function", because you are afraid.

If you see a better way to do what your job calls for, make it known.

Fear is one of our most exhausting emotions. Fear will sap our strength, retard our creativity and rob our joy. The best way to defeat a fear is to confront it by doing that which we are afraid of doing. So, ***go for it!***

Enter your place of work each day with the attitude, "today I will make a difference, I will make it better, I will **make it in spite of** the job, the system, the boss and myself. I will remember that obstacles are those frightful things I see when I take my eyes off my goals."

Go for it...set goals and ***make*** them happen.

Go for it...make one of your goals... ***to work because you want to*** instead of because you are afraid not to. You will be better for it, so will your organization.

ATTITUDE PROBLEM

LACK OF LOYALTY

Loyalty cannot be demanded, loyalty either is or it isn't. Loyalty is defined as: "Steadfast in allegiance."

The person with an attitude lacking loyalty will rarely say anything good about their organization, its management or its contribution to the community. They will look for every way they can to do as little as possible in order to just get by.

On the other hand they will readily spread abroad the negative imperfections of their work place and try as best they can to degrade its community image and community standing. Often when in one of their negative tirades they will be asked by one of the group in their chosen audience, "why do you continue to work there?" Their answer is simple and plausible..."well, you gotta work somewhere, but I'm looking."

These people are chronic complainers about everything and verbal poison pen artists in their organization.

They serve no one but self and develop the reputation as naysayers...worse they become the joke of their cronies as the "grapevine transmitter" of any information they want passed. Hoodwinked or used these persons are to be pitted for they are unaware of the reputation they are making...one who suffers from, "sour grapes."

SUGGESTED ATTITUDE ADJUSTMENT

LOVE 'EM OR LEAVE 'EM

To be a part of an organization is like being a member of the team, or it's like being a part of a family, a member of a church, or an activist group like AARP. The biggest difference is that when you are a part of a organization you are paid money to perform your part.

No family, no church, no activists group, is perfect but if we belong we do support them with time, talent and money. We love 'em or we leave 'em. Most of the time if we hear someone making disparaging remarks about them we readily come to their defense, in short, we actively display our loyalty.

Certainly we should do no less for the organization from whence we derive our livelihood.

The person who will **make it in spite of** is that person who realizes no one twisted their arm to take a job with their organization and no one will twist their arm to stay.

The winning attitude is with that person who feels a loyalty to the organization of which they are a part. The person whose attitude will open the door to success is that person who has enough integrity to either be loyal or leave.

ATTITUDE PROBLEM

COVER MY BACKSIDE

We are all familiar with the ***C.Y.A.*** organizational syndrome. These are the people who never risk, are afraid to initiate and if an when they make a decision it must be covered by mounds of "paper work" which will exclude them from any responsibility.

These are the organizational people to whom spontaneity is a stranger, and their creed is "better safe than sorry."

They fail to act until all their "ducks are in a row" and therefore, miss out on many an opportunity to make things better by immediate action to correct problematic situations.

They have reams of paper work that will absolve them from any responsibility should anything go wrong.

They get the label of "being cautious" at best or "cowards" at worst. To those who are going to make things happen they are "road blocks" and are circumvented.

The CYA person will never join the ranks of those who will **make it in spite of...!**

Why? Because they are too cautious and seek above all to save their own skins.

SUGGESTED ATTITUDE ADJUSTMENT

YOU CANNOT BE SAFE AND SAVER AT THE SAME TIME

The person who will **make it in spite of** is that person who will "strike while the iron is hot" be they covered or not by paper work. Their attitude is to fix the problem then justify why they acted as they did.

They do not seek to be safe but to be a saver. Individuals such as these fully realize ***they cannot be both safe and saver at the same time.*** <u>***To them progress is worth the risk.***</u>

They are more concerned with group success than their individual safety or security.

These persons will face setbacks but they will ultimately **make it in spite of** because their focus and action is for the good of the whole, not the self!

These persons are few and far between but they are worth their weight in gold. By the way, their personal integrity is always intact.

ATTITUDE PROBLEM

LACK OF TRUST

The lack of trust attitude defeats in many ways. It robs of both productive time and energy, thus life. It creates an air of suspiciousness in those who suffer from it.

This attitude disease has several dead give away symptoms:

1. All management decisions are questioned.
2. One of their favorite phrases to fellow workers is, "what are they doing to us now?"
3. Another of their phrases is, "this sounds fishy to me, what do you think?"

The person who suffers from a lack of trust is withdrawn, defensive and inordinately private.

Often their lack of trust leads to their not being trusted.

They constantly seek clarification even to the most self evident reasons for decisions. They want everyone to justify why, not because they want to know, but rather because they are trying to catch someone in a lie, thus validating their mistrust.

TRUST AND BE TRUSTED

Trust is, "To have or place confidence in as being dependable or reliable."

Therefore, trust, up, down and sideways is the cement that holds an organization together.

The person **who makes it in spite of** is the person who will think, but they will also trust. They realize that decisions made by those in authority have been made on the basis of vast amounts of information and data., which are impossible to share with everyone.

Because they trust they will not waste precious time and energy trying to read into each decision some devious motivation. They will just get on with the business of being positive and productive.

They may not understand the rationale for decisions which effect them but they trust them because their attitude is "someone knows more about this than I do."

These are the people who try to calm the fears of others...and because they do, they will **make it in spite of.**

ATTITUDE PROBLEM

LACK OF ASSERTIVENESS

Being taken advantage of by others is no fun. People who suffer from the lack of assertiveness are prime targets for those who would use them for chores no one else wants to do.

These are those persons who will listen attentively to any problem you present but will offer no suggestions or solutions. Instead they will say, "well, anything you want to do will be all right with me because I'm going to be your friend no matter what." There is no help in that.

Have you ever had some problem that was eating away at you and you wanted advice on how to solve it, then finally gotten up the nerve to share it with someone and after you've laid it all out on the table they look at you and say, "what ever you want to do is O.K. with me." This provokes the urge to attack. You are looking for help, an alternative and you get nothing.

The person with a lack of assertiveness has the attitude of non-involvement. They do not actively hinder but they do not actively help either. They will, therefore, not make it in spite of...!

SUGGESTED ATTITUDE ADJUSTMENT

YOU ARE SOMEBODY

When someone comes to you for help or advice they are seeking just that, advice or help. They are so close to the forest they can't see the trees. They are so close to the problem their objectivity is impossible. Realize that what you have to say is important to them.

They have risked sharing with you because they recognize you as somebody who will seek to understand. They believe in your interest. They believe in your honesty. They believe in your integrity. They believe in your objectivity. They believe in you!

Life is lived in isolation and non involvement or being a part of and involved, the choice is yours and will be determined by your attitude.

Being involved is better. Why not? ***You are somebody!***

ATTITUDE PROBLEM

LACK OF HOMEWORK

These are the people who believe in the notion that you leave home at home and work at work. In seminars around the world I have asked class after class to tell me how this is possible, so far, no one has been able to sufficiently answer the question. The truth is that work effects home and home effects work. To try and completely separate the two is impossible.

It is a mistake to leave work and say to yourself..."that's it for today." In reality that's not it for today. This attitude disallows the fact that the same duties and responsibilities you left will be facing you when you arrive in the morning.

The person who lives by the attitude that work and home do not blend will refuse to talk about work to spouse or friends. They miss out on the opportunity to share their work victories and their frustrations...be they vice presidents or lathe operators.

SUGGESTED ATTITUDE ADJUSTMENT

WE WORK FROM SUN TO SUN BUT WORK IS NEVER DONE

Being the manager of a notions retail store, over dinner Carl had bored his wife and children with one his most pressing work problems; running out of sewing machine needles. His wife remarked, "sounds like an inventory control problem."

This simple statement led Carl to a train of thought that resulted in revamping their inventory control for needles, then other items, then a complete revamping of the inventory control system, the result, a chain wide $1,200,000 increase in sales the following year.

This was not homework in the normal sense of the word but for the person who **makes it in spite of** work is never far from being on their mind.

In reality an idea can happen at any time. An idea is powerful. As Aristotle said,"***An idea is greater than a man - an idea is devine.***"

ATTITUDE PROBLEM

NOT THINKING

Unfortunately for all too many persons their jobs are so routinized, whether making widgets on an assembly line or filling out government forms, that they fall into the defeating attitude of not thinking. Rather, they just go through the motions to get the job done.

The results are disastrous. Mistakes abound! Safety suffers! When the job calls for dealing with people in the same way day after day, the customer soon becomes just like a widget, a thing! Boredom is rampant and attention to detail becomes non-existent. The job is filled with tedium and is dreaded daily until numbness sets in.

The problem is, they have just stopped thinking.

Henry Ford said, ***"thinking is the most difficult thing a person can do, maybe that is why so few people do it."***

Thinking leads to ideas and as Aristotle said, ***"An idea is greater than a man,-an idea is devine...!"***

SUGGESTED ATTITUDE ADJUSTMENT

THINK, NO MATTER WHAT, THINK!

Most people don't like to think because it requires attention and effort. However, if there is any one thing that will distinguish the people who **make it in spite of** and those who don't, it is thinking.

When the widget maker is on the assembly line with the widgets they should develop the attitude of thinking, "could it be better, is it right, does it conform to specifications, what is it to be used for, can I speed up the process?" When filling out the form for the umpteenth time think, "can it be simplified, can it be shortened, can I figure out a way to shorten it, is it really necessary at all?"

When dealing with a customer about the same topic as you have dealt with a thousand others on that topic, think, "what do they look like, what is their unique situation, how do they differ from all the rest?" "What can I do to help?"

When faced with any problem the greatest difference between being only reactive and being successfully pro-active is, **thinking**. The person who will **make it in spite of** is the person who understands what ***Voltaire meant when he said:***

***"No problem
can stand the assault
of sustained thinking."***

ATTITUDE PROBLEM

APATHY

There is perhaps no more devastating attitude to personal success than that of apathy, just not caring. The person eaten with apathy will never **make it in spite if** because they don't care whether they make it or not.

These persons are easy to spot, like a weather vane they turn where ever the wind blows. They are committed to nothing, not even self. For whatever reason they have chosen to retreat into a turtle like shell of non-involvement.

When asked for an opinion they have none.

When asked to be a part of a group, they won't.

When asked to make a commitment their indifference is maddening to those around them.

They seem to hold a position on no issue. It appears their only purpose is to exist. Since they seem to believe in nothing, enthusiasm evades them, their direction is determined by the situation of the moment and they live in the eternal now moment.

Those poor souls consumed by apathy will never **make it in spite of** because they will not take a stand one way or the other.

Like a ship without a rudder their destiny is determined by circumstance, not chosen purpose.

SUGGESTED ATTITUDE ADJUSTMENT

FIND A FUTURE AND WORK FOR IT

Apathy about today is a denial of tomorrow.

There is more to life than the moment. The apathetic attitude does not recognize the fact that tomorrow comes and what we do today will determine what the quality of tomorrow will hold.

If you suffer from the apathetic attitude please, for your own sanity, safety and security, find something in the future that you can work toward. It does not matter what it is, as long as it is something that will force you to gain momentum to go forward with determination and purpose.

To be without purpose is to be among the "living dead." The person who **will make it in spite of** denies apathy and lives by the expression of ***Sir Walter Scott:***

"One hour of life, crowded to
the full with glorious action,
and filled with noble risks,
is worth whole years of those
mean observances of paltry
decorum, in which men steal
through existence, like sluggish
waters through a marsh,
without either honor or
observation."

To beat the apathy attitude...find a future and work for it because:

"You will become as small
as your controlling desire;
as great as your dominant
aspiration."

James Allen

ATTITUDE PROBLEM

THE ORGANIZATION OWES ME

The person with this attitude problem has a creed they vocalize with gusto..."more for me."

They want and want and want. To these persons having a job is a right not a privilege.

Mistakenly, somewhere along the way in our culture we have allowed, and I fear even fostered, the attitude of something for nothing. This has led to the development of the individual anticipation of being taken care of, either by government or business, from the womb to the tomb. Thus, there is "the organization owes me" syndrome.

For persons with this attitude self reliance has become obsolete and dependence has become the order of the day. They never ask what can I do for my organization but they constantly chant what they feel the organization should be doing for them.

People with this attitude will never **make it in spite of** because the "organization owes me" attitude lulls them into the false belief that they don't have to do it for themselves in that someone else is responsible for making it happen for them.

SUGGESTED ATTITUDE ADJUSTMENT

GROW UP AND GET REAL

The ***bottom line truth is this: organizations don't "owe" people anything.*** However, when you are a part of an organization from whence you receive your livelihood, ***you owe it*** all you are or shall ever be to make it better. If you can't adopt this attitude, please have enough ***personal integrity*** to ***find yourself a job where you can.***

Enough said!

ATTITUDE PROBLEM

NOT LOOKING FOR THINGS TO IMPROVE...

This attitude is found in chronic complainers who voice their complaints but are willing to live with things the way they are.

To initiate any change is too great a challenge. They reason, "it will take too much effort, too much energy and probably will fail anyhow," so they do nothing.

They are not looking for progress because the avenue to progress, they feel, is always someone else's responsibility.

These are the people who come to work at the appointed time, work and go home.

Their credo is "come weal or woe our status is quo."

When confronted with change they are the first to bellow, "we can't do it that way because we ain't never done it that way before."

These persons are also famous for the ,"if it ain't broke don't fix it," syndrome.

They have a comfort zone and they don't look for ways to improve things for fear the improvements might upset their established comfort zones.

Their **future is a sure thing, extinction.** Not being able to adapt to the progress others will make take place they simply die out.

They will never **make it in spite of, because** they will never make it at all.

SUGGESTED ATTITUDE ADJUSTMENT

IMPROVEMENT IS THE NAME OF THE GAME

The person who will always **make it in spite of** understands, and adopts the attitude, that the difference between success and stagnation is progress.

They further realize that progress in the organizational world is defined as "anything that gives their area of responsibility a greater capacity to perform."

Their constant question with regard to their duties and responsibilities is, "what is a **better way** to do this?, or how can I **improve** it?"

Their credo is, "to take the best of yesterday and couple it the best of today in order to make tomorrow better."

They are not afraid of change or the challenge that comes with it because their attitude is not one of comfort but growth. They seek not the "calf path of the past" but endeavor to make a new trail that will make it clearer and better for all who will follow.

People with this attitude are the persons who will **make it in spite of** because they will take responsibility for themselves and determine their own destiny.

To these people I pass one of my favorite quotes:

"Accept the challenges,
so that you may feel the
exhilaration of victory."

General George S. Patton

ATTITUDE PROBLEM

BEING TOO SATISFIED

The persons with this attitude problem are not going to make anything happen. They are by definition; "content, comfortable, pleased, gratified, delighted and snug." In other words their goals are reached. Such a person has accomplished the ultimate comfort zone. Their horizons are attained and their aspirations are a reality. To say it another way they have nothing further for which to live.

According to this, you show me someone who is satisfied and I will show you someone who is dead, they just haven't laid down yet.

The satisfied person will contribute nothing because to contribute means to "make a change in the essential nature of what you do or a change in the essential nature of how you do what you do." The satisfied person doesn't need or want change in either the what or the how because they "have arrived." But, they have arrived at atrophy at best and stagnation at worst.

At work, if you examine the satisfied person's desk you will find ultimate neatness. They have no irons in the fire because all their irons have grown cold with completion. They used to be a "house afire" but now they are a "burnt out stick."

To most they seem to "have it made." They have position, money and time, but the insides of these persons who "have it made" are hollow and empty. They play too much golf, spend too much time at the nineteenth hole and long for the days when they were busy, dissatisfied and hungry. That time when they were truly alive with activity that meant something and accomplished results that made a difference.

They need an attitude change to rediscover the prime mover of all human progress. Dissatisfaction.

SUGGESTED ATTITUDE ADJUSTMENT

DISSATISFACTION WITH A PURPOSE

Think about it, what is the prime mover of all changes you have made to make progress take place in your life? I'll wager you will discover it was some dissatisfaction. I firmly believe that persons do not change anything in their lives until they become dissatisfied enough with what is...be it personal or business.

Recall relationships for example. Have you ever been in a relationship that was tearing you apart day by day? Well, if you have, you exited yourself from it on the day, the moment, and the hour that the dissatisfaction of staying in it was less than the feeling of loss if you left, and not until.

Dissatisfaction is definitely the prime mover of all progress. The oyster for example does not produce a pearl until its shell is introduced with an irritating dissatisfaction. Therefore, a string of pearls for which we pay a premium price is nothing but the result of a lot of oyster irritations or dissatisfactions.

All business dissatisfactions and irritations are potential points for making progress take place. Persons who will **make it in spite of** understand that it works this way: First, there is some dissatisfaction. Second, they, through gaining knowledge, figure out a better way. Third, they create that better way which they then initiate through persistence, determination and drive. They believe in what they have created and enthusiastically pursue it to completion.

ATTITUDE PROBLEM

UNWILLINGNESS TO GIVE

In life these are those persons who have the attitude that reflects in their behavior, what is mine is mine what, is yours is ours. Psychologically they are best described as being, "anal retentive."

In organizations they are well aware of the fact that information is power, so they seek to gain as much information as possible but they also seek to retain it without sharing it until they can gain something from it.

They know all of the organizational politics and they are master manipulators of the existing "grapevine" to their own benefit.

Since they are primarily takers, when they reluctantly give anything their most important consideration is "what's in it for me?" Like sponges they soak up everything to its minutest detail and feel a sense of power as a result.

These are little people with big ideas and no clue as to how to make their ideas a reality without hurting or "blackmailing" someone else.

These are dangerous people because they don't care who they hurt to get ahead.

Several characteristics they display make them rather easy to identify; (1) You never get a straight answer from them. (2) The information you get is usually "off the cuff." (3) The information is usually from some third party.

These people will never **make it in spite of** because they will be found out and avoided like the plague.

SUGGESTED ATTITUDE ADJUSTMENT

"IT IS MORE BLESSED TO GIVE THAN TO RECEIVE"

This is the person who will assuredly **make it in spite of** in any organization because they are the persons others look to for the correct information. They tell it like it is good or bad.

These are those persons who gladly assist others, who help them and ask nothing in return.

Their assistance is focused on the good of the whole and the benefit of the organization.

Because they are confident and competent they do not have the need to "blackmail" or threaten.

They are concerned more with progress than with power and they believe that the greater amount of information people have the better they will perform..

With regard to "organizational rumor and politics" their rule is this, "if I can't say something good about another, I will say nothing."

With a willingness to give of their time, their talent and their information, these people will become legendary in their own time and will surely **make it in spite of** because they are respected and trusted.

They cooperate and are cooperated with.

ATTITUDE PROBLEM

LACK OF PRIDE IN A JOB WELLDONE

Persons with this attitude problem are in the main, sloppy, slovenly, slow and anything but meticulous.

On the job they create problems with quality, customer satisfaction, customer service and are often responsible for excessive waste, scrap and rejects.

This in turn creates more work for everybody.

The concept of job excellence is not in their vocabulary. They are often hap-hazard in their performance and frequently they are the cause of low morale in their group.

With these people we have tried to correct the problem with programs such as Statistical Process Control and Quality Training concepts, all to little or no avail.

These people will not **make it in spite of** because they lack pride in themselves and that lack of self pride spills over into the work place to create lack of pride in a job well done.

SUGGESTED ATTITUDE ADJUSTMENT

NOTHING LESS THAN THE BEST IS GOOD ENOUGH

This is the creed of those whose pride shows forth in all they do. Theirs is the attitude of ***"if it is worth doing it is worth doing right."*** They feel their work is a direct reflection of their own worth and value. Since they value themselves they also value the quality of what they do.

Pride is defined as, "A sense of one's own proper dignity or value; self respect. Pleasure or satisfaction taken in one's work."

If by some miracle of modern science we could develop a "one a day personal pride pill," the individual productivity problem would be beaten and quality and excellence in all that is done would be, like breathing, a way of life for all.

The person who will **make it is spite of** takes pride in themselves, pride in their organization and pride in what they do.

Suggestion to organizations, build pride in your workforce and your workforce will make you proud of them.

NOT FEELING A NEED TO CONTRIBUTE

The person with this attitude is in a rut they do not realize that the only difference between a rut and a grave is, the grave is closed on both ends.

These persons are as routine as clock-work.

They come in at eight and leave at five. They are very "house broken" individuals. They feel that their showing up for work and going through the motions is contribution enough.

These people will never make it to the ranks of those who will **make it in spite of** , how could they? ***They retired on the job long ago, they just haven't told anyone about it yet.*** These are the people that I have designated as those who are on ***industrial welfare.*** They take from freely but couldn't care less about making a contribution any greater than the perfunctory performance of their assigned duties as contained in their job descriptions.

SUGGESTED ATTITUDE ADJUSTMENT

DETERMINE TO MAKE A DAILY DIFFERENCE

Adopt the attitude that every day you will make a difference in your organization in your area of responsibility and you will make that difference through your own individual contribution. Realize that in an organization contribution is best described as:

"making a change in the essential nature of what you do or a change in the essential nature of how you do what you do."

It may be that you will never change what you do but be on a constant lookout for ways to change the 'how' of what you do. Had others not been doing this from day one we would still light fires by rubbing two sticks together. Until we can all 'walk on water' there will always be a better way. Seek it out and contribute.

People with this attitude will always **make it in spite of** because they understand that to be equal to the challenges of tomorrow we must forge the future today. Their attitude is progressive, so they are those **prized people** who **make progress happen**. Those with this attitude also realize the fact that ***today has validity only as it impacts for a better tomorrow for us all.*** More importantly, these people don't wait for opportunity ,rather, they make their own. To these people ***initiative is a way of life.***

POINTING OUT PROBLEMS AND GIVING NO SOLUTIONS

There is a phenomenon I have observed in conducting seminars around the world, it is that almost everybody is a "expert" at pointing our problems. On the other hand there is an equally universal phenomenon, almost everybody is a rank amateur at giving solutions to the problems they can so readily diagnose.

The attitude of being a **problem finder** without also being a **solution giver** leads to frustration and resignation, frustration that the problem exist and resignation that it never will be fixed. It becomes a defeating vicious cycle.

These will not be among those who **make it in spite of...** because they don't look for solutions, rather, they feel that whatever the problem may be it can't be changed. So, they just live with it.

SUGGESTED ATTITUDE ADJUSTMENT

DON'T COMPLAIN
JUST GO AHEAD AND FIX IT

Somewhere I read the following which I feel is the perfect attitude to adopt for the above to be reality.

"DID
IS A WORD OF ACHIEVEMENT,
WON'T
IS A WORD OF RETREAT,
MIGHT
IS A WORD OF BEREAVEMENT,
CAN'T
IS A WORD OF DEFEAT,
OUGHT
IS A WORD OF DUTY,
TRY
IS A WORD EACH HOUR,
WILL
IS A WORD OF BEAUTY,
CAN
IS A WORD OF POWER."

CAN IS THE WORD OF THOSE WHO MAKE IT IN SPITE OF...!

ATTITUDE PROBLEM

ALLOWING MANAGEMENT TO MISMANAGE

The attitude that believes management can make no mistakes, is wrong. The attitude that management can do nothing right, is wrong. The attitude that management has all the authority and I shouldn't get out of place and say anything, is wrong. The attitude that all "crap" flows down hill, is wrong. The attitude that I must tell management what they want to hear and not what they need to hear is not only wrong, it is cowardly. The attitude that management has all the information, is wrong.

To predominantly hold any one or more of the attitudes above will not allow you to **make it in spite of**, not because of management but because of your attitude with regard to management.

SUGGESTED ATTITUDE ADJUSTMENT

MANAGEMENT IS MADE UP OF PEOPLE FIRST MANAGERS SECOND

As difficult as it may be for some individuals to believe (depending on the type manager they have) managers are ***people first and managers second.*** Managers are neither omniscient, omnipotent nor omnipresent. Managers like you, are human, needing, wanting and imperfect.

The duties of the manager may be different from the bank teller, typist, construction worker or assembly line person and the vast majority want to do a good job, no an excellent job but they need you. They need your input. They need to hear it like it is, because sometimes they don't know. They too, can make mistakes and their mistakes can harm everyone. When they make mistakes tell them...don't blame them...tell them, discuss the mistake and why it was a mistake. If they are worth their salt and confident in themselves and their jobs they will admit it and correct it.

Managers do not want to purposely mismanage. If you allow it without trying to do something about it, you allow the organization to suffer or worse, reach an untimely demise.

The person who will **make it in spite of**, realizes that most all managers are rational and reasonable, so they openly discuss mistakes and their cure, ***for the good of all.***

BELIEF: "YOU JUST CAN'T GET GOOD HELP ANYMORE."

If I have heard it once I have heard it a thousand times around the world from supervisors, management and employee personnel alike, ***"you just can't get good help anymore."*** This is a defeating attitude for the organization, for themselves and for the person or persons to whom they are making reference. ***It is strange but true, what we say about others is what we believe about them and what we believe about them is what they will live up to. It is called "the Pygmalion effect." Put another way, a false belief creates a true reality.***

The person who holds this attitude about their workforce does little to make it more effective and more productive and more efficient. They remind me of the Governor whose state was having constant turmoil in the prison system. When asked what his administration planned to do about it he replied, "We're never going to have a better prison system until we get a better class of prisoner."

Persons who have the "you just can't get good help anymore" attitude will not make it to the ranks of those who **make it in spite of** because theirs is the attitude of those who feel it is a problem of the person about whom they refer not theirs, be they management, supervisor or fellow employee.

GOOD HELP IS MADE NOT BORN...!

"As the twig is bent, so grows the tree." The problem with "good" help is the twig is never bent so the tree does not grow in the right direction. In all my years of formal educational training I was not once subjected to the meaning and value of work itself, were you? I doubt it.

You see "good" help is made not born. Too often too many are conditioned to see work as only a means to an end and not the way to leave their footprint in the sands of time, i.e. making things better for the persons who will follow.

To the person, be it fellow employee, supervisor or manager who will **make it in spite of** question is what can I do to develop good employees? They will then discover there are three major things to question, and then make them right:

1. Does the individual know what their job is?
2. Does the individual know how to do the job?
3. Is something or someone interfering with his or her desire or ability to do the job?

The employee needs to know exactly what you expect of them and you need to know what exactly you expect of the employee. The person who will **make it in spite of** does not expect the employee to be competent and productive and motivated until they have done all in their power to make them that way.

NOT LEARNING FROM MISTAKES

Few things in this life create more individual misery, turmoil and heartache, than that of not learning from mistakes. History proves the truth of the saying ***"if you don't learn from history you are destined to relive it."***

Those who do not learn from their mistakes will fail over and over and over again. Persons with this attitude are hard-hearted and hard-headed. It seems they feel they can do no wrong or commit no error in either judgement or behavior.

Theirs is the philosophy of "luck." They believe that success is simply a matter of luck. And if you don't believe it, ask any failure.

Those who do not learn from mistakes fill divorce courts, juvenile halls, hospitals, prisons, bankruptcy courts and mental hospitals, to mention only a few. They will never be in the ranks of those who **make it in spite of** because these are the people who do not learn from yesterday in order to make tomorrow better. They do make the same mistake twice by doggedly holding on to the belief, "I was the victim and it was somebody else's fault."

SUGGESTED ATTITUDE ADJUSTMENT

A MISTAKE IN OUR HISTORY MEANS A SUCCESSFUL FUTURE

One of the major marks of real maturity is the willingness to admit and learn from mistakes. The person who is wise enough to do this will **make it in spite of** and will never long for what is expressed in the following:

"I wish there were some wonderful place
called the land of beginning again.
Where all our mistakes and all our
heartaches could be dropped like
an old coat at the door and never
be put on again."

Clara Olney

Remember; whoever passed on to us
"live and learn"
passed on really good advice.

Go forth and **make it in spite of...!**

UNDERSTANDING BASICS ABOUT SELF AND OTHERS

In order to alter attitudes in ourselves or others it is helpful to realize certain basic fundamentals that make us think and act as we do. When attempting to change your own attitudes or the attitudes of others please keep the following in mind:

1. A person will stay with an organization as a productive and motivated member only as long as the organization meets most of their real or perceived needs.

2. Wherever a person hurts most is what that person is motivated first to fix.

3. A person does something for only one of two reasons: to gain something or to keep from losing something.

4. The single most significant other in anyone's life is that person from whom they gain most the feeling of being affirmed.

5. One will perform more positively for a person they perceive as significant than they will for a person they feel is an untrustworthy "whimp."

6. The individual has only two basic need systems: (1) Physical needs: Air, Water and Food and (2) Emotional needs: Acceptance, Affirmation, Affection and Achievement.

The implications of these six "basics" are enormous to individual relationships and especially to the successful management of people in organizations to achieve productive results.

<u>EPILOGUE</u>

This book is about individuals, organizations, **attitudes** and work. It was written to show there are some attitudes which defeat us and some attitudes that make us those persons who will **make it in spite of**...! The attitudes that defeat us and the adjustments to those attitudes which, when enacted, will make us winners, have been described. As in all things the attitude you, the reader, choose to adopt is up to you and you alone.

The choices you make depends on your beliefs and your view of life, which in essence ***defines your philosophy of life, and thus your day to day living of that life.*** I teach a course in "Public Speaking" in which one of the assignments is to present a three minute speech on ***"Your Philosophy Of Life."*** For the participants in the session this is the most difficult of the seventeen assignments but it is always the best presentation of the series. It is the most difficult because few have ever given it much thought, and it is the best because they bare their souls which makes it the most sincere and the most convincing. Why? Because they share with the group what they really believe, beliefs which form their values and attitudes and, thus, the attitudes and actions by which they live. ***<u>Where you can identify your negative attitudes you can now change those attitudes to more positive, more productive ones.</u>***

I teach ,"If you can't write or say it you can't do it." So on December 26, 1978 I determined that the best gift I could give my children; Mike , Jeff , Steve and Lisa on December 25, 1979 was a philosophy of life by which to live, with their permission, I share it with you in the hope it will help you to be one who will **make it in spite of...!!!**

A PHILOSOPHY TO LIVE BY

"DO IT YOURSELF"

"HONOR LIVING THINGS;
THERE IS PURPOSE FOR ALL.
ENVY NO MAN.
RESPECT ALL MANKIND; BE COWED BY NONE .
BE BRAVE AND COURAGEOUS ,
NEVER FOOLHARDY OR INDISCREET.
HAVE COMPASSION FOR ALL,
BUT BE DUPED BY NONE.
AFTER CAREFUL CONSIDERATION,
SPEAK YOUR TRUTH
AS YOU UNDERSTAND AND BELIEVE IT TO BE.
NEVER COMPROMISE YOUR INTEGRITY
FOR THE MOMENTS GAIN,
BUT BE OPEN TO CHANGE
IF ANOTHER'S REASON PREVAILS,
OTHERS HAVE BELIEFS TOO, TRIED AND TRUE;
THEY HAVE A RIGHT TO THEIRS AND YOU DO YOURS.
BE PATIENT,
FOR PERSISTENT PATIENCE
HAS CHANGED THE COURSE OF LIVES
AND HISTORY.
ESPECIALLY BE PATIENT WITH THE IGNORANT,
FEARFUL, DOGMATIC AND THE YOUNG,
THEY TOO MUST LEARN.
THE LIMIT TO PATIENCE IS LIMITED BY;
JUDGEMENT, HOPE, AND TIME.
FALSE HOPE IS WORSE THAN NONE AT ALL;
BEWARE THEN LEST IMPULSE
MEAN LOST OPPORTUNITY.
BEWARE TOO, LEST FALSE HOPE ROB OF TIME,
THUS LIFE AND PROGRESS. HAVE FAITH,
FIRST IN DEITY, THEN IN YOURSELF,
THEN IN FELLOW MAN.

*NEVER SELL ANY ONE OF THEM SHORT.
BE JUST BUT FAIR, MIGHTY BUT MERCIFUL,
STRONG BUT GENTLE.
THERE IS MORE STRENGTH IN A FALLEN TEAR
FROM THE HEART
THAN IN ALL THE DEMANDING ANGER THERE IS...!
BARE YOUR FEELINGS FREELY BUT NOT
FOOLISHLY;NOT ON WHIM BUT ON TRUST.
LOVE AND BE LOVED
BUT NEVER BE IN LOVE WITH LOVE.
LOVE NEEDS OBJECT, PERSON PURPOSE,
MUTUAL HAPPINESS TO FLOWER.
WHEN LOVE HAPPENS TREASURE IT
BUT NEVER HOARD IT,
SPEND IT, FOR REAL LOVE CANNOT BE DEPLETED.
ABOVE ALL ...LEARN,
KNOW IN ORDER TO UNDERSTAND,
FOR IN UNDERSTANDING
THERE IS POWER FOR GROWTH.
BUT PERSONHOOD COMES BEFORE POWER...AND
GROWTH TOWARD YOUR MEANING HAPPENS ONLY
AS YOU HELP OTHERS GROW!
DETERMINE TO DIE WITH DIGNITY
RATHER THAN LIVE WITHOUT IT.
LIVE EACH DAY TO ITS FULLEST PURPOSE.
MIMIC NO ONE, BUT WITH CARE
BLEND THE BEST OF EVERYONE
TO DISCOVER YOUR OWN IDENTITY.
ENTHUSIASTICALLY PURSUE YOUR DESTINY, FOR
LIFE IS BEAUTIFUL EVEN IN ITS AGONY.
HAVE PRIDE WITHOUT ARROGANCE,
SHOW CONFIDENCE WITHOUT CONCEIT,
EXPERIENCE JOY; IT IS YOUR RIGHT.*

J. Thomas Miller, III, December 26, 1978

FOR INFORMATION ON SERVICES AVAILABLE FROM LEADERSHIP SEMINARS ASSOCIATES
AND
MILLER'S MANAGEMENT MOMENTS

CONTACT

J. Thomas Miller, III
Leadership Seminars Associates
Miller's Management Moments
610 Elberta Lane
Ft. Mill, S.C. 29715

TELEPHONE (803) 396-8275

REMEMBER

YOUR ATTITUDE MAKES YOU

BUT...
YOU MAKE YOUR ATTITUDE!!!

**THE END
IS BUT
THE BEGINNING**

**SO GO, MAKE IT
IN SPITE OF..!**

Author's Note to the Reader

IT IS MY SINCERE DESIRE THAT THIS WORK HAS REINFORCED MANY OF YOUR ALREADY HELD BELIEFS about the importance of attitudes AND HAS GIVEN YOU NEW WAYS TO "LOOK" AT OLD THINGS...IF YOU CAN FIND THE TIME AND FEEL SO INCLINED, I WOULD GREATLY APPRECIATE YOUR CRITIQUE AND COMMENTS ON THIS WORK. ADDRESS ON PAGE 85 THANK YOU IN ADVANCE. I WILL DO MY BEST TO RESPOND TO EACH OF YOU WHO MAY WRITE OR CALL.

TOM MILLER...

"THE NOBILITY OF WORK"

The whole of human history is written in our ability to make tools and perform meaningful work which meets our needs and upgrades the quality of our lives.

There have been times work was regarded as demeaning, limiting, and not meant nor fit for the socalled "better class."
Nothing could be farther from the truth!
Work gives us a stage upon which we find, and act out our own unique worth and value, as well as allowing us to place an indelible footprint in the sands of time in the history of man's on going agenda.

Our ability to work gives our lives meaning, direction, purpose, expression...that is quite a lot.

Work is the vehicle with which we attach ourselves to the past, to the present, and the tool we use to shape tomorrow's destiny today. Therefore, live by the following formula:
The right attitude X superior performance = success.

Dont just live history, that's too easy, the challenge is to make history, thus, ***Making It in Spite Of...*** "

About the Author

J. THOMAS MILLER, III

As ***Dean of the Management Division*** of Greenville Technical College from 1973 to 1978, Tom Miller was responsible for designing, managing, administering and instructing a curriculum covering all phases of management education and skills. He is a past program chairman and instructor for the ***American Management Association***, past lecturer for the ***University of Southern California Management Safety School*** and served on the training staff for the State of California's ***Police Officers Standards and Training***. He has done training classes and seminars for the New York based firm Frost and Sullivan who provides training sessions for managers internationally. Tom has the unique ability to cut through nationality and cultural differences. His course "Effective Management / Leadership Techinques" has been received with equal enthusiasm in all areas of the ***U.S., the United Kingdom, Germany, Switzerland, South Africa, Kuwait and Canada***.

Presently, Tom Miller is President of Leadership Seminars Associates, a company he founded in 1974 and is now ***internationally recognized*** for its excellence in management training classes, lectures, keynote speaking engagements and seminars. Tom has conducted training sessions for thousands of managerial personnel representing **a vast cross-section of business, industry, and government at all levels.** He uses his exceptional instructional skills to make class sessions meaningful experiences for participants. As a testimony to his results he enjoys a ***92% return engagement rate*** with those organizations for whom he has conducted seminars. Mr. Miller is ***co-author of two previous books, "Every Supervisor A Winner", and "The Secret of Motivation."***

Later this year he will publish his new manuscript *,"The Titanic Syndrome*", a book about ***the "icebergs" encountered in modern marriage, other love relationships***, and those faced in everyday living. His *"**Managements Moments**" **publication is an instructional tool*** helping Supervisors and Managers acheive maximum performance from themselves and their associates in carrying out their duties and responsibilities.

www.ingramcontent.com/pod-product-compliance
Ingram Content Group UK Ltd.
Pitfield, Milton Keynes, MK11 3LW, UK
UKHW040017200726
13854UKWH00001B/252

9 781588 200709